THE HEART OF L'ARCHE

A SPIRITUALITY
FOR EVERY DAY

JOHN E. COCKAYNE, JR.

Other books by Jean Vanier

with Darton, Longman and Todd, London
Tears of Silence (1970)
Man and Woman He Made Them (1988)
Community and Growth (1989)
The Broken Body (1989)
Treasures of the Heart (1989)

with Paulist Press, Mahwah, New Jersey
Eruption to Hope (1971)
Be Not Afraid (1975)
I Meet Jesus (1986)
I Walk With Jesus (1987)
Man and Woman He Made Them (1988)
Community and Growth (1989)
The Broken Body (1989)
From Brokenness to Community (1992)

with The Crossroad Press, New York
Jesus, the Gift of Love (1994)

with Gill & Macmillan Ltd., Dublin
Be Not Afraid (1975)
Followers of Jesus (1975, 1993)

with Griffin House, Toronto
Tears of Silence (1970)
Eruption to Hope (1971)
In Weakness, Strength (1975)

with Hodder & Stoughton
Jesus, the Gift of Love (1994)
The Door of Hope (1995)

with Lancelot Press, Hantsport, Nova Scotia
Images of Love, Words of Hope (1991)
Network of Friends (2 volumes) (1992, 1994)

with Meakin, Ottawa
Treasures of the Heart (1989)

THE HEART OF L'ARCHE

A SPIRITUALITY
FOR EVERY DAY

Jean Vanier

NOVALIS/GEOFFREY CHAPMAN/CROSSROAD

Photos: cover: Stéphane Ouzounoff; p. 14: W P Wittman.
All others: L'Arche.

© 1995 Novalis

Novalis
49 Front Street, East, 2nd Floor,
Toronto, Ontario, Canada, M5E 1B3

The Crossroad Publishing Company
370 Lexington Avenue, New York, NY 10017

Geoffrey Chapman (a Cassell imprint)
Wellington House, 125 Strand, London WC2R 0BB

Scripture quotations are taken from the New Revised Standard Version of
the Bible, © 1989, Division of Christian Education of the National Council
of Churches of Christ in the United States, and are used with permission.

Canadian Cataloguing in Publication Data
Vanier, Jean, 1928
The heart of L'Arche: a spirituality for every day
(L'Arche Collection)
Issued also in French under title: La spiritualité de l'Arche.
ISBN 2-89088-732-4
1. Spiritual life. 2 Caring--Religious aspects-- Christianity. 3. Arche
(Association). 4. Church work with the mentally handicapped.
I. Title. II. Series.
BX2350.65.V36   1995   248.4.8   C95-900381-9

British Library Cataloguing-in-Publication Data
A catalogue record for this book is available from the British Library
ISBN 0-225-66805-X

Library of Congress Catalog Card No.: 95-69127
ISBN 0-8245-1539-0

Printed and bound in Canada.

Contents

INTRODUCTION

In August 1964, inspired and encouraged by
Dominican Father Thomas Philippe, I began to
share my life with Raphaël Simi and Philippe Seux.
Living with these two men with mental handicaps
and with others who, like them, suffer from mental
handicaps, has transformed my life. Before I met
them, my life had been governed chiefly by my head
and by a sense of duty. I had created inner barriers
to protect myself from my fears and vulnerability. In
L'Arche, I began to learn to live from the heart.

Despite some difficult moments, these thirty
years have brought me great joy. My heart has been
opened, my understanding has grown. I have
learned a great deal about the human being's heart
and its need for, but also its fear of, a relationship of
love and communion with others. I have learned
much about the gospel, and about the life and person
of Jesus. L'Arche has been a school of love.

Society regards people with disabilities as "mis-
fits," "sub-human." The birth of a child with a

handicap is considered a tragedy for a family. But in L'Arche we discover that these people have a great openness of heart and capacity for love; they seem to reveal what is most fundamental in all of us. Living with them in community can be difficult, but it also transforms us and teaches us what really matters in life. We may come to L'Arche to help the weak, but we soon realize that, in fact, it is they who are helping us!

Life in L'Arche is demanding, and it involves a degree of sacrifice. Those who come to live in L'Arche have to learn to accept reduced salaries, longer working hours and the loss of certain friendships and cultural activities. But at the same time we gain a great deal: community life, a sense of being loved, a new sense of meaning and purpose in life, and a more integrated way of living in which our faith, gifts and competence are brought together. L'Arche is a place where we can grow and deepen our humanity as well as our spirituality.

God has given L'Arche as a gift to this particular time in history. Today, so much emphasis is put on technology and scientific knowledge that people forget the importance of the heart and of the individual; others sink into depression and despair. Society often seeks to eliminate people who are weak before their birth or through euthanasia, arguing that they are a nuisance and cost too much. Through L'Arche, God reminds us of the essential purpose of human life: out of love, we have been created to love: to use all our energies and gifts to create a more just and loving society, where each person has a place.

Our communities want to witness to the church and to the world that God knows all persons in their deepest being and loves them in their brokenness. God is love. God is goodness, compassion and forgiveness. L'Arche is not a solution to a social problem, but a sign that love is possible, and that we are not condemned to live in a state of war and conflict where the strong crush the weak. Each person is unique, precious and sacred.

L'Arche is a family created and sustained by God. Being a family means sharing one spirit, one vision, one spirituality. This is particularly true of a family created in a response to a call from God, without the natural family bonds of flesh and blood. A spirituality is a way of life that implies choices and a particular ordering of priorities. Each religion has a spirituality, a way of living and growing in union with God. The gospel is the source of Christian spirituality, but there are many ways of living out the gospel.

Throughout history, according to the needs of particular ages and cultures, the Holy Spirit has called forth men and women to create new families, to bear witness to the love of God, the resurrection of Jesus and the gift of the Holy Spirit. In the East as in the West, at the early days of the church, there were the desert fathers and the foundation of monastic families. They developed a spirituality centred on a life of prayer, community life, obedience and liturgy. Much later, Franciscan families came into being. They lived a life of poverty and a belief in the presence of God in nature and in the poor. Other spiritualities have grown up that stressed the importance of integration with and commitment to society. There are spiritualities for marriage, and particular spiritualities for other states of life. Each one has the same foundation: the gospel and the life of Jesus. Each one offers a way to grow in love and become liberated from fear, a path to communion with Jesus and other people.

The Holy Spirit created L'Arche through Father Thomas Philippe to reveal to an age obsessed with achievement that the essential value of each person lies, not in the intelligence, but in the heart. God has chosen to manifest himself in a particular way in people with handicaps, through their weakness and the simplicity of their hearts.

In this book, I want to talk about some of the essential elements of our spirituality that we live daily in our communities throughout the world. I write from my own experience, in my own language, with my own particular sensitivities. Others in L'Arche might write quite differently or emphasize different aspects. This book describes a path to unity, peace, forgiveness and freedom that people with handicaps have given to L'Arche. Other Christians know this path as they share their lives with people who are weak and dependent in other ways:

the elderly, the dying, people with AIDS, people suffering from mental illnesses, etc. L'Arche communities form a new family in the greater Christian family, the people of God.

Some L'Arche communities are inter-faith. In India, for example, our communities welcome Hindus, Muslims and Christians. Each person is rooted in his or her religious tradition. In some ways, Gandhi's spirituality was similar to L'Arche's. He too found God in the poor, the suffering, the rejected; he learned that as we become closer to the poor and enter into a covenant of love with them, we become closer to God. This book, however, deals mainly with the biblical foundations of L'Arche's spirituality: the life and message of Jesus passed down to us through the gospels.

A question of language

Language has evolved a great deal over the last thirty years. People used to talk about the "mentally retarded" or the "mentally deficient." Today we use other terms: "people with learning disabilities" or "people who are mentally challenged." Language evolves according to culture, country and times. Behind the change of language is the desire to affirm that a person with a mental handicap is first and foremost *a person,* who should be respected and given the opportunity to exercise his or her particular gifts.

In this book, I have kept the term "a person with a mental handicap" or "people with mental handicaps." They are truly *people* with all the implications that this word holds. Each person is unique and important. Yet there is difference. Some people come or are sent to L'Arche because of their handicap; others choose freely to come and live with them. The important thing in language is to signify difference while respecting the person.

Sometimes today people have difficulty with the words "the poor" and "the weak." The gospel message talks about the "poor" which is frequently interpreted as the "economically poor." But a person without work and a parent who has lost a child are also poor. The poor person is one who is in need, who recognizes this need and cries out for help. Weakness is frequently considered a defect. But are we not all weak and needy in some way? We all have our vulnerable points, our limits and our handicaps. When we recognize our weaknesses, we can ask for help; we can work together. The weak need the strong but, as we are discovering in L'Arche, the strong also need the weak. In this book I have occasionally used the words "poor" and "weak," even though they go against certain cultural norms that want everyone to be strong.

Special thanks

I would like to thank Claire de Miribel whose knowledge of L'Arche's spirituality made this text clearer and more precise.

My special thanks also to Maggie Parnham who worked hard at improving the English and typing it at the last minute.

Jean Vanier
January 1995

Jean Vanier speaking at Regina Mundi Farm,
Sharon Ontario, in 1990

I

THE MYSTERY OF JESUS

Christian spirituality is founded on Jesus. We in L'Arche are called to live in a special way the mystery of the poverty and weakness of Jesus who came to be with the poor and the weak.

Jesus came to bring the good news to the poor. He set out his mission when, in the synagogue in Nazareth, he applied to himself the words of Isaiah:

The Spirit of the Lord is upon me,
because he has anointed me
to bring the good news to the poor.
He has sent me to proclaim release to the captives,
and recovery of sight to the blind,
to let the oppressed go free. (Luke 4:18)

Through L'Arche I began to understand what the good news is for the poor.

In the time of Jesus, many people were poor, oppressed, blind and rejected. Many lepers suffered, not only the pain of their ulcers, but even more, the pain of rejection. They were regarded as "untouchables"; those who associated with them became impure. Their disease was seen as a punishment from God.

People like these were outcasts, imprisoned in broken self-images and feelings of misery and guilt. They had neither future nor hope.

At the same time others lived in luxury. They had power, prestige and privilege. They lived complacently. Their good fortune and well-being were seen as signs of God's blessing and favour. A wall separated these two worlds: the rich who, on the whole, despised the poor, and the poor who remained turned in on themselves in dejection and sadness. Jesus described the two worlds in one of his parables:

There was a rich man who was dressed in purple and fine linen and who feasted sumptuously every day. And at his gate lay a poor man named Lazarus, covered with sores, who longed to satisfy his hunger with what fell from the rich man's table. The poor man died and was carried away by the angels to be with Abraham. The rich man also died and was buried. In Hades, where he was being tormented, he looked up and saw Abraham far away with Lazarus by his side. He called out, "Father Abraham, have mercy on me and send Lazarus to dip the tip of his finger in water and cool my tongue, for I am in agony in these flames." But Abraham said, "...between you and us a great chasm has been fixed, so that those who might want to pass from here to you cannot do so, and no one can cross from there to us." (Luke 16,19-26)

Jesus ate with rich people like Simon the Pharisee, and Zaccheus. He called them to change, to share their goods with those in need instead of looking down on them. He did not insist that they sell their houses, but he did call them to open their hearts to the poor. After meeting Jesus, Zaccheus decided to give half his goods to the poor. Jesus is very clear when he says:

Blessed are you who are poor,
for yours is the kingdom of God.
Blessed are you who are hungry now,
for you will be filled.
Blessed are you who weep now,
for you will laugh.
Blessed are you when people hate you,
and when they exclude you,
revile you, and defame you on account
of the Son of Man.
Rejoice in that day and leap for joy
for surely your reward is great in heaven;

for that is what their ancestors did to the prophets.
But woe to you who are rich,
for you have received your consolation.
Woe to you who are full now,
for you will be hungry.
Woe to you who are laughing now,
for you will mourn and weep.
Woe to you when all speak well of you!
for that is what their ancestors did to the false prophets. (Luke 6:20-26)

Jesus did not come to judge or condemn, but to gather into one all the scattered children of God (John 11:52). He came to break down the walls that separate the rich from the poor, the strong from the weak, the healthy from the sick, so that they might be reconciled to one another and discover that they are all part of one body.

When Jesus walked the roads of Galilee, people who were weak, sick and poor sensed his goodness and compassion. He loved them. He healed the sick and gave strength and hope to each person he met. He even went into places of ill repute; he was close to those who felt themselves religious outcasts. He spoke to them with kindness, revealing God's goodness and mercy. He wanted to change the way society was organized, not through force or new, rigid laws, but by befriending the powerless and teaching a way of humility and communion between hearts.

The Jewish people were oppressed and humiliated. Under Roman occupation they were living under the yoke of foreign soldiers and the brutal power of the Roman Emperor's representative. Between Jews and Romans there stood a wall of prejudice and hatred.

Jesus did not seek to become a king so that he could create a new, just society in which each person would be properly respected. Rather, he took the downward path of humility in order to become one with the wounded. Paul invited his disciples in Philippi to take the same path:

> Let the same mind be in you that was in Christ Jesus,
> who, though he was in the form of God,
> did not regard equality with God
> something to be exploited,
> but emptied himself,
> taking the form of a slave,
> being born in human likeness.
> And being found in human form,
> he humbled himself
> and became obedient to the point of death—
> even death on a cross. (Philippians 2:6-8)

Jesus invites his disciples not to seek importance or power, even for the sake of doing good to others, but rather to take the lowest place, to serve others like a slave. "God has brought down the powerful from their thrones, and lifted up the lowly," says Mary in her Magnificat (Luke 1:52).

Jesus offers an entirely new vision. God is not just a kind and compassionate being who watches over the poor and calls the rich to share with them, the kind of God we find, for example, in Isaiah:

> Is not this the fast that I choose:
> to loose the bonds of injustice,
> to undo the thongs of the yoke,
> to let the oppressed go free,
> and to break every yoke?
> Is it not to share your bread with the hungry,
> and to bring the homeless poor
> into your house;
> when you see the naked, to cover them,
> and not to hide yourself from your own kin?
> Then your light shall break forth like the dawn,
> and your healing shall spring up quickly;
> your vindicator shall go before you,
> the glory of the Lord shall be your rear guard.
> Then you shall call, and the Lord will answer;
> you shall cry for help, and he will say, Here I am.
> If you remove the yoke from among you,
> the pointing of the finger, the speaking of evil,
> if you offer your food to the hungry
> and satisfy the needs of the afflicted,
> then your light shall rise in the darkness
> and your gloom will be like the noonday.

The Lord will guide you continually,
and satisfy your needs in parched places,
and make your bones strong;
and you shall be like a watered garden,
like springs of water,
whose waters never fail. (Is. 58:6-11)

Jesus does not just serve the poor, he becomes one of them. The Word becomes flesh; the All-Powerful becomes a defenceless child who awakens love. His words, his actions, his whole way of being, disturb people, above all, powerful people. They refuse to listen to him or to accept him: they even seek to kill him. Finally they give him over to the civil authorities, the Roman leaders. Jesus is condemned to death and dies in total abjection. He is mocked by all. The man of compassion becomes a man in need of compassion, a poor man. Jesus overturns the established order: he urges people not simply to do good to the poor but to discover God hidden in the poor, to discover that the poor have the power to heal and free people.

Nakibule and Anne, L'Arche-Uganda

II

A SPIRITUALITY CENTRED ON THE MYSTERY OF THE POOR

The two worlds today

The two worlds that existed in the time of Jesus still exist today in every country, city, town—and every human heart. The rich are those who, believing they are self-sufficient, do not recognize their need for love and for others. There is a rich person in each of us. There are the materially, culturally and even spiritually rich, who, self-satisfied, live in luxury, caught up in wealth, power, and privilege. They have more than they need, and yet they constantly seek still more! They look down on those who are different or weak. And then there are always a great number of people living in poverty and misery, unable to cope: the homeless, the unemployed, the victims of abuse, those who suffer from mental illness or from mental or physical handicaps. There are the elderly who are lonely and neglected, the mentally unstable, people trapped in broken self-images. There are those who suffer malnutrition and famine; there are refugees fleeing from hatred, violence and war.

Jesus' message today is the same as ever: he came to gather together in unity all the scattered children of God and give them fullness of life. He longs to put an end to hatred, to the preconceptions and fears that estrange people and groups of people. He longs to create in this divided world places of unity, reconciliation and peace, by inviting the rich to share and the poor to have hope. This is the mission of L'Arche and of other communities: to dismantle the walls separating the weak from the strong, so that, together, they can recognize they need each other and so be united. This is the good news.

A competitive society

Because our Western societies are consumer societies that encourage individualism, they are also competitive societies. In school, children are taught that they must strive to come first; that they must win in order to be admired; that they can only hope to get a prestigious, powerful, well-paid job when they grow up if they are successful when they are young. In practically every walk of life, people struggle to climb the ladder of success in order to have more: more money, more influence, more recognition.

There are good things about competition. It helps people develop their talents and do their best. Without competition or the urge to be well-known and admired, humanity's progress in many areas would have been slower. The search for excellence develops excellence. But it also has negative aspects. For each person who wins, how many lose, feel discouraged and cease to develop their gifts? Unable to climb the ladder of success, they fall down into the pits and lose self-confidence. Those who have succeeded in climbing the social ladder tend to despise those who have not managed to do so.

I was part of this competitive world. I wanted to be "on top." I saw little value in those who were "on the bottom," even if from time to time I did try to help people in need, doing what I could to attract them upwards, encouraging them to seek success and a better standard of living.

In 1963, thanks to Father Thomas Philippe, I discovered the world of people "on the bottom." In visiting institutions, asylums and psychiatric hospitals, I discovered a whole new world of people with mental illnesses or mental handicaps. It was a world of despair and madness. These people had been hidden away far from the rest of society, so that nobody needed to be reminded of their existence. Shut up in rooms together, some turned round and round all day for want of something better to do. The dormitories were sometimes well organized, but there was nothing at all personal in them. The staff were often good-hearted, but they did not have time to give people individual attention. The men and women suffering from mental handicaps were often neglected, left to themselves or sometimes even oppressed. If they did try to revolt—and they often had every reason to do so—they were severely punished. This crushed not only their aggressiveness, but also their hope.

It would be wrong to condemn those who created these institutions, or the staff who worked in them. They were simply the products of a culture that regarded people with limited intelligence as pathetic creatures incapable of real suffering. Some institutions did take good care of their people and treated them with love, affection and respect. But even in those places, no one really believed that people with mental handicaps could grow and become more autonomous, or offer anything to others.

I met Raphaël and Philippe in an asylum near Paris where they were locked up behind enormous walls. It was a dismal place. The people who lived there had no work, and the place was filled with cries of violence and depression. As a child Raphaël had had meningitis, which had impaired his sense of balance and left him unable to speak. It was much the same for Philippe. Both had been sent to this asylum when their parents died.

I bought a small, dilapidated house in Trosly, a village in northern France, and invited them to come and live with me. That is how the adventure of L'Arche began.

The adventure of L'Arche

As I began to live with Philippe and Raphaël, the first thing I discovered was the depth of their pain, the pain of having been a disappointment for their parents and others. One can understand their parents' reaction to them. Which parents would not be distressed and angry to discover that their child would never be able to talk, walk or live like others? Parents whose children have handicaps suffer deeply. But children who have handicaps suffer deeply, too. Raphaël and Philippe had incredibly sensitive hearts. They had been deeply wounded by rejection, by the lack of consideration shown them by those around them. Because of this, they sometimes became very angry, or escaped into a world of dreams. It was quite clear that they had a great need for friendship and trust, and to be able to express their needs to somebody who would really listen. For far too long, nobody had been interested in listening to them or in helping them make choices and become more responsible for their lives. In fact, their needs were exactly the same as mine: to be loved and to love, to make choices and to develop their abilities.

As our friendship grew and deepened, I became increasingly aware of the cruelty of our societies that promote the strong and reject the weak. This rejection seems to be deeply ingrained in our cultures and institutions. Even the church often fails to recognize the value of people with handicaps. It is as if our societies cannot admit that these people are fully human and that they suffer terribly from rejection and contempt. Admittedly, church and society recognize that it is important to "do something" for them and their distraught parents, but rarely do they see that these people truly have something to offer in return.

Being counter-cultural

Over the years, I have come to realize the extent to which sharing our lives with people suffering from mental handicaps is counter-cultural.

Soon after L'Arche began, I came across the passage in Luke's gospel in which Jesus says:

When you give a luncheon or a dinner, do not invite your friends or your brothers and sisters or your relatives or rich neighbours, in case they may invite you in return, and you would be repaid. But when you give a banquet, invite the poor, the crippled, the lame, and the blind. And you will be blessed, because they cannot repay you . . . (Luke 14: 12-14)

I had heard this text often, but its full force had never struck me. Suddenly I realized that it described what we were living at L'Arche as we sat down at the same table as Raphaël, Philippe and others. Sitting down at the same table meant becoming friends with them, creating a family. It was a way of life absolutely opposed to the values of a competitive, hierarchical society in which the weak are pushed aside. I began to realize just how counter-cultural the good news of Jesus is.

Although they were good Christians, some parents of assistants were mortified by the idea that their sons or daughters chose to live at L'Arche. Had their children chosen to be priests or nuns, they would have been proud of them, but they considered their choice to live with people "like that" beyond the pale. Some said: "It's such a waste that my son is in L'Arche; he could have done something really useful with his life!"

But although the life we were living was so counter-cultural, I was nevertheless encouraged by Father Thomas, and by a number of psychiatrists and people involved in the French government and social services. They appreciated the importance of treating people with mental handicaps as people first, of helping them make choices and of providing them with a warm, supportive home, fully integrated into a town or village where they could build up friendships with the neighbours and the local community. They, too, believed that big institutions, which were more like prisons, should be avoided. Most people with mental handicaps are not sick and do not need constant medical treatment; they need to live in surroundings adapted to their needs, in which they can grow, develop and find meaning in their lives. I was struck by how often the human sciences came to the same conclusions as the gospel. Competitive, individualistic, materialistic societies detract from our humanity; the message of Jesus is profoundly human.

Befriending the poor awakens and transforms the heart

Making friends with Raphaël and Philippe and living a covenant—a sacred bond—with them implied an enormous change in the way I approached life. My education had taught me to be quick and efficient, and to make my own decisions. I was, first and foremost, a man of action rather than a man who listened. In the navy, I had colleagues, but no real friends. Opening ourselves to friendship means becoming vulnerable, taking off our masks and letting down our barriers so we can accept people just as they are, with all their beauty and gifts as well as their weaknesses and inner wounds. It means weeping with them when they weep and laughing when they laugh. I had created barriers around my heart to protect it from pain. In L'Arche, I was no longer climbing the ladder of human promotion and becoming more and more efficient and important. Instead I was "descending," "wasting time" with people with mental handicaps, so that together we could create communities, places of covenant and communion.

Obviously, I needed to do some things for Raphaël and Philippe. They needed help to become more autonomous, to learn to make choices and assume more responsibility for their lives. But this was not the most important need. Above all, they needed to escape from a sense of isolation, to belong to a community of friends and form bonds of love and communion. I had to learn what really loving someone, entering into communion with them, meant. Loving someone means, of course, wanting to do things for them, but more essentially it means being present to them, helping them to see their beauty and value, and trust themselves. Loving involves letting others see my own poverty, and giving them space to love me. It was especially vital for Raphaël and Philippe to find friends, since they had experienced so much rejection and had very negative self-images. They were convinced that they were "no good," that they had only been sources of trouble and pain to their families and others. I had to fight against these convictions by showing them the joy I felt in their existence and in sharing my life with them.

As I touched the fragility and pain of people with mental handicaps, and as their trust in me grew, new springs of tenderness welled up in me. I loved them, and was happy with them. They awakened a part of my being that had been under-developed, dormant. Through them, a new world began to open up for me, not the world of efficiency, competition, success and power, but the world of the heart, of vulnerability and communion. They were leading me on a path towards healing and wholeness.

To be a friend to the poor is demanding. They anchor us in the reality of pain; they make it impossible for us to escape into ideas or dreams. Their cry for solidarity obliges us to make choices, deepen our spiritual lives and put love at the heart of our daily lives. It transforms us.

This growth in friendship with the poor also reveals our own inner conflicts. It is so easy to try to escape from its demands, and be seduced by activities or personal projects that seem more pressing, or by other distractions and pastimes that diminish our solidarity with the poor. Leading a truly Christian life—welcoming the poor, living the spirituality of L'Arche—is a real struggle. We cannot be faithful in this struggle unless we receive the gift of the Holy Spirit in times of silent prayer, when we rest quietly in the love of Jesus.

As I grow in friendship with people who are weak and powerless, I am beginning to discover in them qualities of the heart that I find less often in people who have devoted their energies to success. Of course, I should not generalize. Every person is unique, and has his or her own gifts and wounds. The people we have welcomed in L'Arche, however, have a great gift of simplicity in relationship. They are not governed by social conventions. They welcome visitors with joy, and make no distinction between those who are important in the eyes of the world and those who are not. They are not interested in anyone's profession or rank, but they are perceptive about people's hearts. They do not wear masks; they express both joy and anger quite naturally. They live in the present moment, and are not caught up in a longing for the past or in dreams about the future. This seems to make it easier for them to forgive and make peace. All these qualities make them men and women who welcome, celebrate and enter into relationship. Free from the urge to compete and succeed, many of them radiate joy. This joy is not clouded by past hurts, but seems to flow from them. They seem to have a greater wholeness than many people who are more intellectually or practically gifted. They show us a path of love, simplicity and joy.

Discovering my own wounds

If, at times, some people with handicaps awakened a new tenderness in me, and it was a joy to be with them, at different moments others awakened my anger and defensiveness. I was frightened that they might touch my vulnerability. I felt agitated and ill at ease with them, just the opposite of the peace and openness I needed to be present to them. It is hard to admit to the darkness, fears, anguish, confusion and psychological hatred in our own hearts, all that hides our past hurts and reveals our inability to love. If we love only those who love and affirm us, is that really love? Is it not simply self-love? How can we learn to get out of ourselves and be open to those who cry out their anguish, who need to be loved but upset us and awaken our own anguish? For those who, like me, have always been able to do what they like and have always succeeded, it is difficult; at the same time it can be a real source of salvation to discover our poverty and our powerlessness, and to be confronted by failure.

I had to accept my own difficulties and poverty, and look for help. Faced with my anger and inability to love, I came into contact with my own humanity and became humbler. I discovered that I was frightened of my own dark spots, that I always wanted to succeed, to be admired and ready with the right answers. I was hiding my poverty. It is easy to see the flaws in others and judge them. It is more difficult to accept our own flaws. How quickly we try to justify ourselves and blame others instead of humbly admitting our own weakness and sin.

Can we be loving and compassionate with Raphaël and Philippe, and accept their poverty and woundedness if we cannot accept our own? Living with people with handicaps and becoming their friends force us to come down off our pedestals and recognize our common humanity and our own difficulties in loving.

I realized that to become a friend to people in need, I needed to pray and work on myself, with the help of the Holy Spirit and good spiritual accompaniment—someone who would walk with me and share my life. I had to learn to accept myself without any illusions. I had to discover how to forgive *and* my own need for forgiveness. Little by little, the weak and the powerless helped me to accept my own poverty, become more fully human and grow in inner wholeness.

Being attentive

When you are with people who suffer from mental handicaps, you cannot be in a hurry. It takes time to listen to them and understand them. Efficiency is not their strong point! They find their happiness in presence and relationship; their rhythm is the rhythm of the heart. They oblige us to slow down and enter into relationship.

Listening is first of all an attitude. Without judging them we try to understand the pain, desires and hopes of other persons. By listening attentively, we give them a sense of value and help them to grow in self-confidence. Many people suffer when they sense that others do not want to understand them. They close in on themselves. But if someone takes time to listen to them attentively, they begin to open up.

It is not just a question of listening to words, but also to the non-verbal, to body language. Raphaël hardly spoke at all. I had to learn his language, the meaning he gave to the few words he could say. I had to learn to interpret his bodily gestures, his tears, his smiles, his touch, his cries of anger that sprang from frustration. People with mental handicaps express themselves more through their bodies than through words. We have to be very attentive to this simple, concrete language to grasp the pain and the problems as well as the desires behind it.

Giving someone a bath is one of the strongest experiences at L'Arche. When a person is naked, he or she is particularly vulnerable. One has to be attentive to the reactions of the body, to make sure that the person draws the greatest possible benefit from this special time of relationship. Great respect and tenderness are necessary. I had never given a bath to anyone before I came to L'Arche. When I came to do so, I was reminded of Paul's words: ". . . do you not know that your body is the temple of the Holy Spirit within you?" (1 Cor. 6 19). This little, fragile, naked body is God's dwelling place. My own body is God's dwelling place, too.

If I am too self-centred or always trying to prove myself, I will find it difficult to listen to others. Listening to the words or body language of another implies a kind of dying to myself; it implies an openness to receive what he or she wants to give: sometimes darkness and rebellion, but also inner beauty.

At L'Arche I have learned what unconditional listening is. If a person is violent, deeply disturbed or depressed, the assistants meet with the medical team to try to understand what the person is living, what he or she is trying to say through the violence, to understand the root of the pain. No moral judgments are made. Of course, some limits have to be put on destructive behaviour, but there must always be discussion so we can understand and help these persons make choices and leave their world of darkness.

As I learn to listen, I learn not to judge people according to rules or to what is "normal." Rather, I try to identify their pain and help them take a step forward. If we ask too much of someone, he or she will feel paralyzed and possibly guilty. If we do not ask enough of them, they will not grow. Listening has also helped me detect more quickly the masks that so-called "normal" people wear to hide their limitations, wounds and inner pain. Listening without judging has helped me grow out of my prejudices, the fruit of my education, and have a greater appreciation of people from different cultural and religious backgrounds. When others sense that you want to understand them and be close to their hearts, they too let down their barriers and begin to trust.

But it is not always easy to listen and be close to other persons. They may challenge the things we believe in. To listen attentively to others means taking them into your heart, trying to understand and love them. It means risking to look clearly at the weeds as well as the good seeds in the field of their lives and naming them, without making the person feel guilty. It also means respecting and trusting them. Sometimes when we uphold the importance of moral values and social norms and customs, we find it difficult to be close to people who, for various reasons, do not observe these standards. Yet when we listen to people who are addicted to drugs, or those serving time in prison, we begin to understand their inner wounds and pain, and their difficulties in observing such laws or appreciating these values. If we befriend recent immigrants, we begin to gain insight into the pain they experience as they face a new culture and language. We suffer when others judge or condemn these people without taking time to understand them. Similarly, as we become close to people with mental handicaps, our value system changes. A new world opens up for us in which kindness, gentleness and compassion come before achievement and power. The spirituality of L'Arche necessarily changes our attitudes; we become humbler, more open. Community life has the same effect.

The poor, chosen by God

When we listen to the poor with open hearts, without prejudice, we discover that they can be prophetic. People suffering from mental handicaps do not know God in an intellectual, abstract way, but they can sense when they are loved. When children know that they are loved, they are peaceful. When they feel unwanted, they are in pain. They learn through contact with their hearts, their bodies, their senses. Isn't it the same for all of us and especially for people with severe mental handicaps who have few abilities and are never admired for their achievements?

In my community, we welcomed Eric, a young man who was blind and deaf. He could not speak, walk or eat by himself. He came to us from the psychiatric hospital where he had suffered the separation from his mother who loved him very much, but was unable to care for him. He had also suffered from passing through many hands that touched and handled him, often without love or any real commitment. He had developed a very negative self-image. When he arrived in L'Arche, our task was to find ways to show him that he was lovable, just as he was, that we were happy he was alive. He used to come to the chapel with us. Those close to him during the eucharist remarked how peaceful his face was. How could he know he was in the chapel, the house of God? Only through a sense of the presence of God, an inner peace given to him. The mystery of the incarnation is that God comes to us and reveals to us the breadth and the depth of the Trinity's love; God lives in us and loves us. God's presence is revealed to our hearts through the gift of the Holy Spirit. As children of God, we are called to receive this gift of presence and to open our hearts to this love. People who have highly developed intellects often try to reach God through their minds and thoughts. People who have limited intelligence are more open to a simple presence, a heart-to-heart relationship of communion and love. They receive God in the peace of their hearts, although they are unable to put their experience into words. If Eric could have described what he lived during the eucharist, he would probably have said: "I was filled with deep peace and joy."

Sometimes it is difficult for intellectually gifted people to understand this type of knowledge that comes from the heart. They think it is of little value because it is too emotional. They forget that it is the most fundamental form of knowledge in each of us: that we felt loved or rejected by our parents forms the basis of our psyche. The experience of falling in love and the joy we feel when we are loved by or love others both come from knowledge that flows from the heart.

This does not mean that people with handicaps do not need to be taught. Teaching has its place. The most important knowledge, however, is the knowledge that comes directly from a heart-to-heart relationship with Jesus in which they sense how much they are loved and are called to grow in love. With candles, music, the word of God and silence, we need to create an atmosphere that helps each person become quieter and more open to this presence of Jesus in their hearts.

A few years ago, everyone in our house spent two days on retreat. When I asked Didier what had touched him most during the retreat, he said: "When the priest spoke, my heart was burning." I'm sure he would not have been able to tell me exactly what the priest had said. But the music of his voice and his words filled with the love of Jesus were like channels through which the Holy Spirit had touched Didier's heart, giving him a deep sense of peace and joy.

Some people find it difficult to believe in the value of this kind of knowledge of the heart; it may seem too childish or sentimental. Perhaps they themselves lack faith. Or perhaps they are confused by the paradox they see in people with mental handicaps: even though they may be prophetic, they still behave in strange, sometimes self-destructive ways. We forget that God comes to us in the deepest part of our beings, at the source of our life, the innermost heart, hidden behind and beyond the more apparent psychological wounds and barriers.

Paul was conscious of this mystery when he wrote to the Corinthians that "God chose what is foolish in the world to shame the wise; God chose what is weak in the world to shame the strong. God chose what is low and despised in the world . . ." (1 Cor. 1: 27-28).

Jesus touches this same mystery when he speaks of the king who offers a wedding feast for his son (Matthew 22). "Good," well-established people refuse his invitation. They have other things to do; they are too busy. So the king sends his servants out into the highways and byways to invite the poor, the lame, the sick and the blind—all those who are normally excluded from society because of their handicaps. "So the wedding hall was filled with guests" (Matthew 22:10). The poor are open to love; their greatest thirst is for love.

When Jesus said "Blessed are the poor..." (Matthew 5:1-12) on a hill overlooking Lake Tiberias he gave a guide to life, a charter. People gifted with intelligence and knowledge are invited to choose this way of life. Those who are weaker, particularly people suffering from mental handicaps, have no choice. They *are* poor in spirit; many are humble and gentle; they weep because they know pain; they thirst for justice, partly for themselves; many have pure hearts; many are persecuted and can become instruments of peace. Their very being manifests the presence of Jesus, poor and humiliated. That is the reality of their state of life. They can choose either to accept it or fall victim to it; that is the mystery of their freedom.

The fact that they have open, spontaneous hearts does not mean that people with handicaps do not have to struggle and make real efforts in life. They need help, formation and the right support so they can accept themselves more fully just as they are, grow in faith and live, not in an imaginary world, but in reality. During the retreats or formation sessions we have organized in L'Arche and Faith and Light, we help people with mental handicaps look at some fundamental areas: mental handicaps, sexuality, death, the presence of God. These sessions bring some of them a real freedom and inner maturity.

Jesus: present in the poor

Jesus tells us that whoever welcomes a little child in his name, welcomes him, and whoever welcomes him, welcomes the Father (Luke 9). The little child symbolizes all those who cannot cope by themselves, who need somebody to be with them and help them most of the time. Jesus identifies himself with outcasts, with strangers, with those who are hungry, thirsty, naked, sick, imprisoned when he says: "... as you do to one of the least of my brothers and sisters, you do to me" (Matthew 25). What a mystery of faith! How can Jesus, the Word of God, be present in Eric with all his poverty? Is it really possible that when I am in contact with Eric I am in contact with God?

Jesus's identification with the poor remains one of the greatest and most incomprehensible mysteries of the gospels. How can God who is all powerful, all beautiful and all glorious become so powerless, so little, so weak? The logic of love is different from the logic of reason and power. When you love someone, you use her language to be close to her. When you love a child, you speak and play with him as a child. That is how God relates to us. God becomes little so that we will not be frightened of him, so that we can enter into a heart-to-heart relationship of love and communion.

The Word became flesh to reveal what is most precious in each one of us: our hearts, our thirst to be loved and our capacity to love, be kind and compassionate and give life to others. What is most important is not our knowledge or influence, but the love hidden in our hearts, which permits us to use our knowledge and gifts to serve others, to give life and to build faithful covenant relationships. That is why Jesus identifies himself with the weak who cry out their need for love and who call people together in communion. The mystery is that our God is a hidden God. Our God is not a God of rules, regulations and obligations or a master teacher who wants to impose a path of salvation. Our God is a God of love and communion, a heart yearning to communicate to another heart the joy and ecstasy of love and communion that exist between the Father, Son and Holy Spirit.

Loic often sat on my lap at evening prayer in La Forestière. This quite small, weak man, who could not speak although he was forty years old, would sit there quietly. He looked at me; I looked at him. It was a deep moment of communion one with the other. We are told that St. John Vianney, known as the "Curé d'Ars" noticed an old farmer who used to sit for hours in the church. When the saint asked him what he was doing, the farmer replied: "He looks at me and I look at him." We have moments like that with our people who, like Loic, are deeply handicapped; moments of contemplation filled with peace and stillness in which "he looks at me and I look at him," healing moments that unify our hearts and minds.

By identifying himself with the poor and the weak, Jesus reminds us that he identifies with all that is poor and weak in each of us. We are called to become more open, trusting, child-like and filled with wonder. Each person is sacred, no matter what his or her culture, religion, handicap or fragility. Each person is created in God's image; each one has a heart, a capacity to love and to be loved.

Consecration

Throughout the ages, Christian churches as well as the other great religions have always valued the call of some people to consecrate their lives completely to God. These people have always been seen as privileged witnesses or signs of God. They are the hermits, men and women living in contemplative monasteries, people who give their lives totally to

Jesus; priests, nuns, religious and lay people who live their celibacy as a gift in his name. Their celibacy announces the eternal wedding feast of God with all of humanity. In the Old Testament, prophets speak of God as "the Spouse" and the people of God as "the betrothed." In the New Testament, John the Baptist calls Jesus "the Bridegroom."

Through baptism, each person's heart belongs to God. Some people, however, are called to manifest this gift of their belonging in a special way and through a particular way of life. The gospels seem to reveal to us another aspect of consecration: the mystery of the poor consecrated to God through the sacred "oils" of pain, rejection and weakness. When Paul says that God has chosen the weak, the foolish and the rejected, or when Jesus, in Matthew's gospel, describes the kingdom of God as a wedding feast to which all the poor, the lame, the sick and the blind are invited, they confirm that the weak have a preferential place in the heart of God. Jesus himself was rejected and outcast; he identifies with the rejected, the outcasts. Is that not the gospel's new order that replaces the old? We in L'Arche are beginning to touch something of the mystery that people like St. Vincent de Paul grasped when he said: "The poor are our teachers."

This does not mean that exclusion or rejection are in accordance with God's will. On the contrary! They are the fruits of sin and hardness of heart. The gospel shows, however, that God welcomes in a special way those whom society rejects.

The mystery of pain

To eat at the same table with suffering, rejected people can be painful. In our community in Santo Domingo, we welcomed Luisito. He was born with a severe mental handicap. His mother lived in a shanty town, in a small hut made of wooden planks. She used to bring Luisito to beg in front of the church. He could not walk or talk. When his mother died, the people in the parish took turns caring for him, washing him, bringing him food. They tried to find a home for him. They heard about L'Arche and prayed for a L'Arche community in their parish. When a community opened in Santo Domingo, Luisito was the first person we welcomed.

It is not easy, however, to live day after day with someone like Luisito who is full of anger, darkness and depression. People who have been rejected tend to close in on themselves and refuse to communicate. Seeing themselves only as victims, they lock themselves up in their own pain and in a world of dreams. When they come to L'Arche, they are invited to open up, relate to others and let down their barriers of protection. That is not an easy transition. At first, the poor will resist any change; they will cry out their anguish, their anger and their violence. When Luisito first arrived, he refused to eat with the others at table: he was used to sitting on the ground and eating with his fingers. He had never done any-thing by himself; others had always helped him. The community tried to help him become independent, more responsible for himself. Each day was a struggle between the strength of our hope for him and the force of his despair.

Luisito has been with us now for ten years. He has not made much progress, but he has found a family and friends. He has started to walk and to work a bit in the workshop. We understand him better, though our relationship with him is still quite fragile. Even if he has opened up a bit, he remains very wounded. Much anger and sadness are still hidden deep in his heart. It takes a great deal of effort for him not to remain discouraged but to get up each day, to walk, work and live with others. Living with Luisito, bearing with his anger and trying to understand his changing moods is quite demanding. L'Arche has given him a home and a new life, but the pain and the challenge of living with him day after day and carrying his anguish remain.

Living with the poor and eating at the same table is not a utopia. It involves conflict and struggle. People suffering from mental handicaps can be quite self-centred. We need to struggle against everything that keeps them closed in on themselves, to help them open up and not be governed by fear and depression. These struggles are painful. We need the support of community life as well as the help of professionals.

A few years ago, I went on holiday for the month of August with a group of fifteen people from L'Arche. Our life together was quite simple, but quite demanding. Several men and women in the group had severe handicaps and we had to do all the cooking and cleaning as well as help them. Since I used to get up very early, I would leave the house and go to morning prayer at a nearby monastery. It was a time of peace and silence for me. Afterwards the monks gave me breakfast. Then, around eight o'clock, as I walked back to the house, my heart felt heavy. After the peace and quiet of the monastery, I was going back to the daily routine of making breakfast, waking up Loic, giving him a bath, waking up the other assistants. As the days went by, I sensed in myself more and more feelings of heaviness and sadness. Yet with the monks I felt so good! I realized that I had to look at my own vocation and accept it more fully, not live in dreams or inner conflict. I had to realize that Jesus had not called me to live the life of a monk according to the rule of St. Benedict, but to find him in the poor, with my people in a daily life made up of little acts of love and service. Jesus had called me to L'Arche.

As we share our lives with the powerless, we are obliged to leave behind our theories about the world, our dreams and our beautiful thoughts about God to become grounded in a reality that can be quite harsh.

That is where we meet God, God who is Emmanuel, God-with-us. There God is present, hidden in wounded humanity, hidden in the pain of our own hearts.

The poor: a mystery of faith

It is easy to understand the need to be generous, to fight for justice against discrimination and poverty. We must do all we can to help teach people with handicaps to learn and take a full part in life. But we must also learn to walk with those who will never be healed, who remain imprisoned in their anguish and weakness. They need friendship and community. They need us to reveal to them their beauty and their preciousness. The gospel teaches us something completely new: that through their suffering and poverty, these people have something particular to offer. They carry, in their very beings, the mark of God and the presence of Jesus (Matthew 25).

L'Arche's spirituality is not chiefly about doing things for the poor, but about listening to them, welcoming them and living with them a covenant— a relationship of fidelity rooted in Jesus' fidelity to the poor—to help them discover the meaning and purpose of their lives.

The poor reveal to those who come to be with them how to live compassionately on the level of the heart. They evangelize us. They show us the way of the beatitudes. A gradual transformation takes place in the hearts of those who come to live with them. They discover their own poverty. They discover that the good news of Jesus is announced, not to those who serve the poor, but to those who are themselves poor. The poor lead them from generosity to compassion, and help them take to heart the words of Jesus:

Be merciful, just as your Father is merciful;
Do not judge, and you will not be judged;
do not condemn, and you will not be condemned.
Forgive, and you will be forgiven. (Luke 6: 36-37)

We gradually discover that people suffering from mental handicaps, and all those on the bottom rung of the social ladder, present us with a paradox. From the point of view of faith, those who are marginalized and considered failures can restore balance to our world. It is said of Jesus: "the stone that the builders rejected has become the very head of the corner" (1 Peter 2: 7). Similarly, if we welcome those who have been rejected, they can transform us. This is the gospel and the new order instituted by Jesus. To be radically transformed, to live with this new love, we need the gift of the Holy Spirit, eyes of faith, a hope and love flowing from the heart of Jesus who gradually transforms our hearts. The transformation in our hearts and in the way we relate with the poor is slow and beautiful. It takes place as we enter into community life.

Dick and Bill at L'Arche-Tacoma

III

A SPIRITUALITY LIVED
IN COMMUNITY

The community is a body

L'Arche's aim is to create communities where people suffering from handicaps can live together with those called to be their friends. The challenge of our communities is to bring together in unity people who are talented and strong, and people who are poor and marginalized.

In his letter to the Ephesians, Paul writes:

[Jesus] is our peace.
in his flesh he has made both groups into one
and has broken down the dividing wall,
that is, the hostility between us . . .
that he might create in himself one new
humanity in place of the two,
thus making peace,
and might reconcile both groups to God
in one body through the cross,

thus putting to death that hostility through it.
So he came and proclaimed peace . . .

(Ephesians 2:14-17)

Jesus' work is to destroy the barriers, prejudices and fear that separate people with handicaps from "normal" people, so as to unite them in a single body. It is the complete reversal of a hierarchical society in which the powerful, the influential and the privileged are elevated, and the weak and poor are put down. Those who are weakest form the heart of the body instituted by Jesus, in which competition no longer exists. Here each person has a place; no one is superior to anyone else. Each person is unique and essential.

In his first letter to the Corinthians, Paul describes this body, which is in fact the church and every Christian community, where every person has a particular role to play.

But as it is, God arranged the members in the body, each one of them, as he chose. As it is, there are many members, yet one body. The eye cannot say to the hand, "I have no need of you," nor again the head to the feet, "I have no need of you." On the contrary, the members of the body that seem to be weaker are indispensable, and those members that we think less honourable we clothe with greater honour, and our less respectable members are treated with greater respect;

whereas our more respectable members do not need this. But God has so arranged the body, giving the greater honour to the inferior member. . .   (1 Cor. 12: 18-24).

We do not know to whom Paul was referring when he spoke of "those members that we think less honourable," those whom one hides away or, as at the beginning of this same letter, "the foolish, the feeble, the outcast." But people with mental handicaps perfectly fulfill his criteria. So often through the ages, they have been hidden away. Paul says that they are necessary to the body, and that they must be treated with special honour. They are important; they have a role to play in our communities and in the church. L'Arche aims to be a body where the weak and the strong are united.

Many types of communities direct their main activities outside the community. Their members teach, care for the sick, campaign, announce the good news. In monasteries, life is centred on prayer and liturgy. At L'Arche, however, the main emphasis is on welcoming people, caring for them, working and living in community with people suffering from handicaps who form part of the community. This kind of life, lived in communion with people who are weak, is the source of healing and liberation for assistants as much as for those with handicaps.

Through this daily life with the poor, Jesus enables us to participate in the communion that he enjoys with the Father. As we share the same table and become friends with people suffering from mental handicaps, people who have suffered marginalization, we achieve unity, reconciliation and peace. We grow in divine tenderness. We discover the forgiveness of Jesus and become a symbol of the wedding feast of heaven.

This is why unity is all-important in a L'Arche community. The spirituality of L'Arche echoes Paul's words to the community at Philippi. Each person is called to be an instrument of unity, without which everything collapses:

> If then there is any encouragement in Christ, any consolation from love, any sharing in the Spirit, any compassion and sympathy, make my joy complete: be of the same mind, having the same love, being in full accord and of one mind. Do nothing from selfish ambition or conceit, but in humility regard others as better than yourselves. Let each of you look not to your own interests, but to the interests of others.
>
> (Philippians 2:1-4).

The ideal community, in which there is no rivalry and each one finds his or her place, is not something that can be achieved once and for all. It requires a daily struggle. Difficulties in relationships, jealousies, anger and fear all spring up very quickly in community life. One starts to ignore certain people. People can be living together in a house and yet pass one another like ships in the night.

It is not easy to enter into community life when competitiveness has been bred into us, when we have grown up to try to be the best, to get increasingly good results, to prove ourselves and try to be admired. Often people develop this need to shine and be admired as a way of soothing anguish and lack of self esteem. But the urge to shine runs contrary to the spirit of cooperation and communion that is at the heart of community life. Entering into this way of life involves real grief. No one is asked to give up his or her whole life or personal opinions, but everyone must be ready to listen to others, seek unity and not impose their way of looking at things. Community living implies cooperating with others and sharing decision-making with them. This means spending time in meetings that can seem long and demanding. Some might feel that it would be much easier and more efficient for house leaders to make decisions by themselves. But if they did, they would fail to respect others, especially the humblest. Living in community means trying to help each person be responsible for him- or herself. Meetings allow all persons to express themselves and listen to others. They offer opportunities for unity to develop.

Community living and the search for unity demand a constant effort to be attentive to and respectful of others, especially those whom we find less agreeable. They demand an effort to accept differences and to live forgiveness daily.

This search for unity is rendered more difficult in L'Arche because of the extreme diversity of all its members. A L'Arche community is a people on a journey. Among these people are those with mental handicaps and those who chose to come and be with them; those who are celibate and those who are undecided about celibacy; those who are married; those who live in the homes and those who have other roles in the community, in the workshops or administration; those given to adoration who live in the community house of prayer; board members and friends who come to help. Then there are all the differences of age, education, culture, gifts and capacities; people are limited or handicapped in different ways; people are on different stages in their faith journey. And finally there are all those differences that stem from the length of time people have been in the community.

Unity in all this diversity comes through those with handicaps. They are at the heart of the community. Through their thirst to be loved and accepted, through the depth of their trust flowing from their weakness, they bring people to oneness and give our lives and our communities their fundamental meaning. This is accomplished through faith and trust in God, through the love that flows from the heart of the Trinity, which opens the heart of each one and gives them new strength to overcome selfishness and work for unity, peace and reconciliation.

Love through small things

After spending time at L'Arche, many assistants agree that living a simple life with people with handicaps has transformed them. Frequently, they have grown up in a world of conflict and competition in which they had to put on masks and be tough. At L'Arche, they learn to drop their defenses, to be vulnerable, to be themselves. Although it is demanding, living a practical life close to other people seems to make them happy. Sometimes, the same assistants who say that L'Arche has transformed them also say that they cannot stay. I remember an assistant who had been at L'Arche for two years telling me that, although he had never been so happy in his life, he had to leave. That many people find themselves in this position shows that community life, though beautiful, involves struggle and grief. The media—especially television—breed a longing for novelty, powerful experiences, grand gestures. To remain faithful to small things without having first made one's fortune seems regressive.

So many marriages break down these days. Could this be because people are afraid of the boredom of the daily routine? They are often stressed out by the hurried, distracting elements that make up their lives—commuting, superficial friendships, the constant blare of the television—and by their inability to cope with their anguish and the difficulties they face in relationships. They no longer know how to find joy in small things. A daily routine consisting of meals, washing, gardening and simple friendships seems too dull and unproductive. If one is going to stay at L'Arche and live this kind of life, not just for a few months or years but for a whole lifetime, one needs to discover a spirituality of love through small things.

The community life we live at L'Arche with people who are weak is rooted in simple, material things: cooking meals, spending time together at table, doing the washing-up, the laundry and the housework, helping meetings to go smoothly, organizing the house so that it is a happy, welcoming place: thousands of little things that all take time. It also means looking after the needs of the weaker people: giving them baths, cutting their nails, helping them buy clothes and looking after their money. In the gardens or the workshops it means doing the best one can with the resources available.

These little things are often seen as insignificant and valueless. But all these small gestures can become gestures of love that help create a warm atmosphere in which the communion of hearts can grow. In this way, community life becomes a school of love.

In community life, it is obviously necessary to have people who are in charge, people with vision who help keep the community unified. But the less conspicuous people also play an essential role: they love tenderly, take time to live with people, give them baths, prepare their meals. Because they live so close to the people with handicaps, they are instruments of love.

L'Arche communities try to be loving, happy places. There is a great temptation to allow ourselves to be seduced by big things, riches, success, power, possessions and privileges. But if we devoted all our energies to these things, it would be easy to forget about human beings, about the need to create places of love and real friendship.

In his first letter to the Corinthians, Paul reminds his disciples that, without love, the search for great things leads nowhere.

If I speak in the tongues of mortals and of angels, but do not have love, I am a noisy gong or a clanging cymbal. And if I have prophetic powers, and understand all mysteries and all knowledge, and if I have all faith, so as to remove mountains, but do not have love, I am nothing. If I give away all my possessions, and if I hand over my body so that I may boast, but do not have love, I gain nothing.

Love is patient; love is kind; love is not envious or boastful or arrogant or rude. It does not insist on its own way; it is not irritable or resentful; it does not rejoice in wrongdoing, but rejoices in the truth. It bears all things, believes all things, hopes all things, endures all things

(1 Cor 13:1-7)

Recovering hope

Our societies are becoming increasingly fragmented. The natural centres of friendship and community, such as parishes and villages, are breaking up. People go their own ways, pursuing their own particular projects and pastimes. People have their friends, and their friendships can quickly become exclusive. The poor are excluded from them.

Is it not vital today to create places of unity, where people really communicate with and open up to one another, and together find out what their lives are really all about? Too many people have lost confidence, not only in themselves, but in society and the human race. Wars, reports of corruption, greed and inequality all reinforce the idea that human beings are evil, that we live in a jungle where people must fight for themselves and where generosity and love are rarely found. To many people, faithfulness in marriage seems impossible. The divorce rate shows this. Some forms of feminism seem to confirm that men are intrinsically bad, and that no communion is possible between men and women.

We all need to recover trust and hope: to rediscover the fundamental beauty of the human heart and its capacity for love. L'Arche communities try to bear witness to the fact that love is possible, that, as individuals and as a society, we are not condemned to selfishness. Like all Christian communities, L'Arche communities want to witness to a belief in love, a belief that human beings can put aside their egoism and open themselves to others. This is their mission in society. Just as a lamp must not be hidden under a bushel, but must shine for everyone in a house (Matthew 5), so our communities must enable others to find hope and live lives of love, sharing and rejoicing in the gift of life. This is why all true communities are called to be integrated into their neighbourhoods and open to those living around them, particularly to the poor, the needy and the suffering. This simple daily way of life in which we are really united to others has universal significance. It helps us to discover that the smallest thing we do for a brother or sister can in some way affect the world.

Descending into humility

Jesus took the downward path of humility. It led him to meet people who were poor and isolated, and to enter into communion with them. Jesus did not seek to free people through changing the law, but through helping them to grow in trust and faith. If we trust Jesus, and try to live in communion with him, he gradually frees us from the fear and selfishness that are inside us governing our lives.

Jesus calls his disciples to follow him on the downward path. "For all who exalt themselves will be humbled, and those who humble themselves will be exalted" (Luke 14:11). He asks us to take the lowest place and become humble, not to imprison us in negative self-images, or make us victims, incapable of responsibility towards our brothers and sisters, but to follow him so we might find him in the poorest of our brothers and sisters—the ones who are always in the lowest place. He invites us to eat with them and open our hearts to live a covenant with them. This is why Jesus gives us the Holy Spirit, who changes our hearts of stone into hearts of flesh. He gives us a new power that reveals itself in our weakness: "My grace is sufficient for you, for my power is made perfect in weakness" (2 Cor. 12: 9).

Jesus knows that we have a tendency to try to assume power and control others. In each of us there is a little latent dictator. Some parents want to completely control their children. Religious dictators oppress others in the name of truth and religion. Those in power often rejected the prophets of the Old Testament. The religious leaders killed Jesus. Jesus had strong words for those who used religion to achieve personal glory and who oppressed the poor without listening to them. There is always a danger that people who are generous will become self-satisfied. There is a danger that they will become involved with weaker people simply in order to have power over them. There is a danger that they will desire admiration for their good deeds. Jesus spoke of this danger in one of his parables:

> "Two men went up to the temple to pray, one a Pharisee and the other a tax collector. The Pharisee, standing by himself, was praying thus, 'God, I thank you that I am not like other people: thieves, rogues, adulterers, or even like this tax collector. I fast twice a week; I give a tenth of all my income.' But the tax collector, standing far off, would not even look up to heaven, but was beating his breast and saying, 'God, be merciful to me, a sinner!' I tell you, this man went down to his home justified rather than the other; for all who exalt themselves will be humbled, but all who humble themselves will be exalted."(Luke 18:9-14)

Imagine the fury of the religious leaders when they heard this parable. They thought that Jesus was trying to undermine their authority, whereas all he wanted was to call each person to recognize his or her own poverty.

The evening before he died, during the paschal meal, his last supper, Jesus took off his clothes and, in the tunic of a slave, began to wash the feet of his apostles. They were astonished, shocked. Peter protested. He could not bear the idea of Jesus, the master, kneeling before him and washing his feet like a slave. After he had put his clothes back on, Jesus explained what he had been doing. He had set an example so that they in turn should wash the feet of others: "If you know these things, you are blessed if you do them" (John 13:17).

Jesus knew the dangers that await his disciples: religious pride and the desire for spiritual power. There was a risk that they would compete with one another in seeking power. The unity between the disciples would then be wounded. And if their unity broke down, it would be hard for people to believe in the truth of their message. On the contrary, Jesus said, "By this everyone will know that you are my disciples, if you have love for one another" (John 13: 35). He prayed that his disciples might be one so that the world might believe in his message of love.

Jesus called his disciples to humility and little-ness. He called them to become like small children, not to seek to prove that they were in the right and that others were wrong. He called them to be with the poor, those without a voice, and through them to live in communion with him, just as he lived in communion with the Father. Pride destroys community; humility helps to build it up. Humility means seeing in the beauty of others the gift of God; it means recognizing the darkness in ourselves, the self-satisfaction behind our good deeds, our longing to take first place. It means recognizing that we need Jesus to free us from this pride that is inside all of us.

Humility means accepting our place in the body of a community and respecting the place of others. It means obeying others and serving them. Humility means recognizing the importance of doing small things for the community. Humility also means having the courage of one's convictions and being fully responsible so that the community can be more loving and true.

By being in communion with Jesus, who is gentle and humble of heart, we can be freed of our tendencies to judge and condemn others, and live humbly with the humble and build with them places of peace and love, places of hope in a wounded world.

Recently an assistant who has been at L'Arche a long time said to me: "I am lucky to be able to just *be* in my house. If I were in charge it would not be like this, but as it is, I can be with people, give them their baths, play with them. I have time to pray, I feel completely relaxed." This is what the downward path means. The way of L'Arche is a way of humility.

Community life: a source of life

Living in community involves much grief. It is a hard and demanding life, but it also brings deep joy and a new freedom. Community life is a source of nourishment.

Entering into community life means giving up a particular kind of independence and personal suc-

Agnès da Silva on the guitar

cess. It means allowing the barriers with which we protect ourselves to fall so that we can allow that which is most fundamental in us to emerge: the vulnerability of our hearts, and our ability to live in communion. As this happens, each person discovers that they are loved for what they are, with all their gifts and weaknesses. All can become fully themselves, without masks, and discover gradually an inner unity. When we have found our place, when we belong to a family, we discover a new security that brings with it the grace of inner peace. We discover our fruitfulness.

In community we learn to welcome differences and to live forgiveness. We live the joy of witnessing to love and compassion. At L'Arche, the assistants have much to endure. They are sometimes tired; there are tensions. But there are also moments of relaxation and celebration. I had never laughed so much before I came to L'Arche. There is the joy of being with very simple people who communicate through humour and peace. There is the joy of being with brothers and sisters who love one another and call one another to fidelity. There is the joy of knowing that we are loved by God in this simple daily life.

Lucia and Armando from Il Chico,
the L'Arche house in Rome

IV

TRUSTING IN GOD
WHO WALKS WITH US

The work of God

When I welcomed Raphaël and Philippe I had no particular plan or precise ideas. I knew nothing about people with mental handicaps, but I had been touched by them in the asylums and institutions I had visited. I wanted, for the sake of Jesus and the gospel, to help them find a more human and Christian life. I had no idea of how a L'Arche community should be organized. As the days went by, I began to understand Raphaël and Philippe's needs and discover what community really meant. I think it would be difficult to find a founder less capable than me. I tried to live each day as it came. Father Thomas was always there to advise and encourage me. I was naive, but determined. I wanted to work for Jesus and for his kingdom. I tried to be attentive to the way in which Providence was guiding me precisely because I did not really know what I was being asked to do!

I am more and more convinced that God has supported and guided L'Arche over the years to reveal to society and the church the place and value of people with mental handicaps—particularly at this point in history when their lives are threatened because people are asking whether they should be alive at all.

When I look at the seed that was planted in the ground on August 4, 1964, and the tree which it has since become, with L'Arche communities all over the world; when I see the beauty and blessedness of so many of the people suffering from handicaps and of so many of the assistants who have come to share their lives with them, I know that this is a work of God which has sometimes been achieved in spite of me. My role was to welcome events as they came and let them guide me. Later I discovered that my ignorance and poverty at the beginning of L'Arche helped me be more attentive to God, and let him guide me from day to day. Had I had a clear plan, I might have been less ready to welcome God's plan.

The necessity of insecurity

At the start, all God's works bring with them this insecurity and poverty that allow us to be more genuinely open to God's action. Then, through the action of Providence, people and money begin to arrive. When people, money and structures are plentiful, the community is in danger. It is easy for it to think that it has less need of God, and to consider itself self-sufficient. Life becomes comfortable, and enthusiasm wanes. Those who get in the way are excluded. People are less present to others; they think more about themselves.

This was the history of the people of Israel. Abraham trusted. He left his homeland and set out into the unknown. Gradually a people grew up, with its own laws and structures and king. The people acquired a certain fame, riches, knowledge. The temptation grew for the people of Israel to want to be big and strong like the surrounding peoples, who were self-sufficient. Depending on God became too insecure; they needed riches and an army to defend themselves and be secure.

At L'Arche, we will avoid this movement from insecurity to security and then to decadence only if we remain alert to three things: fidelity to the poor who cry and disturb, the quality of community life, and trust in Providence. It is not enough to have one founder of L'Arche or of any other community. Each leader is called to re-found the community. The people of Israel had kings and prophets. We need people to look after things, and to look after them well. We also need prophets who remind us of the community's meaning and vocation today and communicate a new flame and a new ardour to ensure that God's plan is fulfilled.

If we are faithful to the needs of the poor and to community life, we will remain open to the prophetic inspiration of the Spirit. People with handicaps know how to disturb us. They disturb us all the more when they sense a lack of real attention and truth. Lack of money and assistants keeps us insecure and forces us to remain open to others and to God. Crises in the community—those of the people with handicaps but also those of assistants: illnesses, accidents, conflicts—demand of us not only human wisdom and the development of appropriate structures, but also constant recourse to God's help. A crisis is an unexpected poverty that calls us to rediscover what is really essential, to rediscover trust and love.

Dependence on God can bring with it weariness and fear. In every community, and in every individual, there are tendencies to seek security, possessions and an organization that will foresee and control all. It is possible to have a false abandonment to Providence in which one seeks merely to cover up one's shortcomings, human failings and lack of reflection through prayer and abandonment to God.

L'Arche needs human wisdom and competence. We need to take care of our communities competently; we need good doctors and psychologists. But the purpose of all these things is to enable us to better respond to the cry of the poor, to allow ourselves to be disturbed by them, and to announce again and again the good news of Jesus.

Remaining open

The nature of a community's dependence on God is determined by whether it is young and small, or larger and more structured. Young and small communities are frequently prophetic in their poverty and spiritual needs. Big communities need to turn to God in order to remain prophetic, to continue to grow in love and to meet new challenges in responding to the cry of the poor.

Recently, a French bishop confessed to me how difficult it was to start up new things in his diocese. The priests and other church officials were already rather overworked, and money was always short. The reaction of his diocesan council was always: "How can we start new initiatives when we have neither the people nor the resources?" I can understand this reaction. Prudence urges us to strengthen the things we already have. The bishop added: "It seems to me that we have to be attentive to the Holy Spirit, and to find new resources and new vocations through new initiatives."

We need to dare to take the lead, be discerning and start new things. The history of the church is a history of constant renewal. New families grow up; new kinds of spirituality appear. This renewal challenges the existing order. New ideas, new communities and new approaches always provoke resistance.

How can we make sure that we are not so caught up in things which already exist that we allow no space for anything new?

The gospel reveals the absolute opposition between God and mammon. In a community based on faith, either one accepts a certain poverty and insecurity to enable God to work, or one refuses this dependence, littleness and poverty, and seeks the means to control things completely: that is mammon.

Isaiah says that openness and trust in God who leads us are essential in any community that wants to welcome the poor:

Do not fear, for I have redeemed you;
I have called you by name, you are mine.
When you pass through the waters, I will be with you;
and through the rivers, they shall not overwhelm you.
when you walk through fire you shall not be burned,
and the flame shall not consume you.
For I am the Lord your God,
the Holy One of Israel, your Saviour.
Because you are precious in my sight,
and honoured and I love you.
Do not fear, for I am with you.

(Isaiah 43:1-5)

Jesus calls us to live in complete trust and to allow God to lead us:

> Therefore, I tell you, do not worry about your life, what you will eat, or about your body, what you will wear. For life is more than food, and the body more than clothing. Consider the ravens: they neither sow nor reap, they have neither storehouse nor barn, and yet God feeds them. Of how much more value are you than the birds! . . . . If God so clothes the grass of the field, which is alive today and tomorrow is thrown into the oven, how much more will he clothe you—you of little faith! And do not keep striving for what you are to eat and what you are to drink, and do not keep worrying. . . . your Father knows that you need them. Instead, strive first for his kingdom, and these things will be given to you as well.

> Do not be afraid, little flock, for it is your Father's good pleasure to give you the kingdom.
> (Luke 12: 22-24; and 27-32)

We need to allow ourselves to be led by God who walks with us on our journey. Some aspects of L'Arche's organization seem impossible: living with people who are weak and poor, allowing ourselves to be disturbed by them, creating communities with them. What folly! We are defying our fundamental selfishness! Love is impossible! But God manifests his glory in making the impossible possible. Through the impossible God reveals divine power and enables us to become witnesses of the resurrection, of the Father's love for the small and weak.

Today, many L'Arche communities have the money they need to run smoothly. This money comes partly from gifts. Providence provides. Yet L'Arche is short of assistants. Sometimes, the assistants we have are stretched to their limits. There is a great temptation to hire assistants attracted by the idea of a salary rather than by a real desire to live the spirituality of L'Arche. At the beginning, I thought we were short of assistants because L'Arche was a young, little known organization. Now I believe that the shortage of assistants is an essential part of our life. It worries and wearies us, but it forces us to be open and constantly welcoming. A community that welcomes poor people will always be poor. We would really love to have plenty of perfect assistants. We would love to be in a position of security. But it will never be like that. Our weakness is like that of the people of Israel: to live and survive, we need, not only love and faith, but also a kind of poverty that keeps us dependent on God. Only by being like children, dependent on the

Father's love, waiting for him to give us all we need, we will be able to carry on with our journey. "Blessed are the poor in spirit, theirs is the kingdom of heaven."

Pope John Paul II at a meeting of the priests
of the L'Arche community

V

A SPIRITUALITY ROOTED
IN THE CHURCH

The place of L'Arche in the people of God

When the Lord called Moses on Mount Horeb, he said to him:

> I have observed the misery of my people
> who are in Egypt;
> I have heard their cry on account of their
> taskmasters.
> Indeed, I know their sufferings,
> and I have come down to deliver them
> from the Egyptians and to bring them out of that
> land
> to a good and broad land,
> a land flowing with milk and honey . . .
> So come, I will send you to Pharaoh,
> to bring my people, the Israelites, out of Egypt.
>   (Exodus 3: 7-10)

The bible shows us how much God cares for people. It allows us to know the love of God revealed in Jesus, the Word made flesh.

All biblical history—from the time of Genesis, through Abraham, Moses and all the prophets until the life, death and resurrection of Jesus and the descent of the Holy Spirit on the apostles and the beginnings of the church—reveals a God who watches over humanity and longs to lead us to inner freedom and peace. But biblical history is also the history of a people who fear God, who allow themselves to be seduced by riches and pride, who turn away from the love and power God wants to show them, so that they can be transformed and become instruments of peace and love.

We are all loved by God, but the gospel shows us that the poor, the weak and the marginalized have a special place in God's heart. Just as God called Moses to free the people from slavery, so God calls and sends the assistants of L'Arche to welcome those who are oppressed and suffering rejection because of their mental handicaps. God opens the hearts of assistants to their cry and to the anguish of these weak people. And the mystery is that these people, with all their fragility and weakness, transform the assistants, evangelize them and call them into the heart of the gospel.

Jesus, the new Moses, came to lead his people towards the Father by showing them the path of love and forgiveness. He came to give his disciples the

Holy Spirit, the Paraclete, the Spirit of truth, to enable them to leave their prisons of pride and self-ishness and open their hearts to universal love. But to receive this gift of love and this new power of the Holy Spirit, we need trust. This is what faith means: trusting in the promises Jesus made to his church.

Since the beginning of the church, the Holy Spirit has guided God's people. Throughout the ages, the good news has been announced to the poor; a new life has grown in their hearts. But there have also been struggles to extinguish the good news and to turn the people of God away from the truth that disturbs the powerful. The poor have often been pushed aside.

The spirituality of L'Arche is rooted in the church, the body of Christ. Like all Christians, we are called to live in hope. Like all Christ's disciples, we are called to receive God's gifts and to take part in remembering the death and resurrection of Jesus in the eucharist. We are called to live from the word of God, the body of Christ, called to live in communion with Jesus just as he lives in communion with his Father.

The spirituality of L'Arche is one way of travelling towards God, of living the beatitudes and the gospel of Jesus. To live this spirituality fully, we need to be united with the body of Christ, the church, and with her pastors. We need to work with them so that the whole body of Christ can share in the gift we have received, and so that we can receive other gifts. The body needs to be united, and to rejoice in the gifts God manifests, at the same time as it humbly recognizes its weaknesses, and neither judges nor criticizes.

L'Arche should not be closed in on itself. It should be a part of the whole church. The presence of priests and ministers in our communities is a sign of this. How easy it is in our communities to forget the promises of Jesus! It is easy to be so caught up in the daily routine that one forgets that people with handicaps are a sign of God's presence. It is easy to forget what is most essential: the communion, the covenant we have been given in Jesus. Our possessions and our bodies, instead of being instruments of grace and communion with Jesus, take up all our attention. We rely on our own power or become caught up in our own angers and depressions, rather than rely on Jesus. Rather than build a community founded on the poor, a sign of the love of God, we create a little institution in search of security and recognition. The work of God can very easily be choked, the signs of God extinguished. To bear witness to the gospel, L'Arche needs to drink from the source of life flowing from the church.

Our communities should play their part in the neighbourhoods in which they are situated and be open to those living around them and to friends. They should be integrated into their parishes and their local churches. The parishes are living cells of the body that is the church. We need to work hard so that they become beautiful, alive, living fully the riches within them. We need to take our places in local churches, to be open and, through our lives together, bear witness to the fact that love is possible and that a person who suffers from a mental handicap has a gift to offer others. We need to receive with wonder the gifts of others, and be in communion with different religious authorities.

Christians divided and yet in communion

L'Arche is a Christian community, but many people who come to live with us are not particularly open to the Christian faith. While some are people with faith and a love of liturgy, others are not attracted by regular religious practice. When it comes to prayer and communion with God, each person is called to find his or her own way. All, at whatever stage they are on their journey, are encouraged to open themselves to others by living a life of fraternity, sharing, welcome, generosity and forgiveness. Diversity is a treasure. The important thing is that we should create a kind of life in which all persons, at their own pace, can grow in the love of God and interior peace.

In 1969, a L'Arche community was founded in Canada by an Anglican couple, Steve and Ann Newroth. In 1970, a community that welcomed people from both Hindu and Christian faiths was founded in India, in Bangalore, by Gabrielle Einsle. Very early in its life, L'Arche developed an interdenominational and inter-faith dimension. We had welcomed people with mental handicaps, not because they belonged to a particular religion but because they were suffering rejection. This led us down a road of ecumenism and inter-faith sharing. Intrinsic to the spirituality of L'Arche is a love that respects others, whatever they are like, with their strengths and their beliefs. This means helping people grow in acceptance of themselves and their own history, and in the love of God and of others. And because L'Arche does not want to set itself apart from the rest of society, all persons, according to their desires and potential, need to be rooted in their own church or religious tradition.

In trying to be attentive to the human and spiritual needs of each of its members, L'Arche has been increasingly drawn into God's plan for unity: the unity of all human beings and of all Christians. Jesus' great longing is that all should be one, as he and the Father are one. Divisions, which lead to oppression, hatred and wars, wound the heart of God. People suffering from handicaps show us the way to unity through welcome, reconciliation and forgiveness.

When L'Arche started up in Muslim or Hindu areas, I realized that the tears and sufferings of a mother faced with a severely handicapped child are the same, whatever her religion. We share a common humanity. We are all God's people. We all have vulnerable hearts, capable both of loving and of being loved. We can all grow in love and gradually free ourselves from the prisons that enclose us in ourselves.

This vocation to unity is demanding. It demands a certain maturity of heart to be able to welcome and respect others in their particular journey of faith, and to discover that, beneath our differences, much unites us. This is possible only if we are firmly anchored in the love of God and meet each one's heart with respect and love.

Growing in love

The spirituality of L'Arche is both profoundly human and profoundly divine. It is like a seed planted by God in the soil of our beings. The soil needs to be tended, the seed needs to be watered and fed. If the soil is too hard, the seed will not be able to develop.

Life at L'Arche is demanding. It is hard enough leaving one's family and job, and the freedom to do what one likes. It is harder still to remain faithful through the years. Like all Christian life, it is a continual growth in love for which we need a gift of God. It demands that we allow ourselves to be constantly pruned. Over the years each of us has developed defence mechanisms and prejudices through which we defend ourselves from others and from suffering. In the deepest parts of our beings, each of us has hidden fears that, consciously or sub-consciously, govern the way we think and behave. Each of us has barriers that stand in the way of our loving some people, and lead us to form bonds with others. God's work is to prune us and dismantle our defence mechanisms so that our hearts can be open to the Holy Spirit and to divine love. God's work is to progressively penetrate our unconscious world, our inner world of guilt, confusion and anguish, to free us, heal us and lead us to wholeness.

It takes a long time to discover unity in ourselves so that we can be a source of unity for others; to welcome our wounds so that we can welcome those of others. It takes a long time to drop our masks and accept ourselves as we are with all our limitations, so that we can accept others. To carry on walking down this road we need to be attentive to God's call and Jesus' promises, and to make choices that bring with them the acceptance of loss.

Few of the people suffering from handicaps had chosen to be at L'Arche. For most of them, there was no alternative. Little by little they have come to accept community life which, we hope, answers their deepest needs. After a time, some of them, like Michel, choose L'Arche for themselves. "I could now call myself 'Michel Arche,'" Michel said one day, "because L'Arche has given me life."

Some assistants come to L'Arche in response to a call from God to live a covenant with people with handicaps. Others come for shorter or longer periods of time to find meaning in their lives. Gradually, they discover the world of tenderness and faith in the gospel; their hearts are touched. Transformed, they leave L'Arche to carry on their journey elsewhere. Those whose vocation it is to live at L'Arche discover in the people with handicaps a source of life, a treasure of tenderness. Jesus compares the kingdom of heaven to a treasure hidden in a field. The person who finds this treasure sells all that he or she has to buy the field.

If we are to grow in love and remain faithful to Jesus hidden in the poor, and faithful to this vocation to unity, we need a certain discipline. Like athletes who want to win, we need to find the right way to look after ourselves. We cannot remain faithful unless we are nourished with the gospel, with the Body of Christ, and with the communion we find with him through prayer. We need to benefit from the help that spiritual masters through the ages have offered to lead us towards God. There are many pitfalls on the way. We need wise accompaniment.

Some assistants feel themselves called to live their vocation with a life companion, and to start a family. Without living with people suffering from handicaps, they are fully members of the community. Their union as a couple is strengthened and nourished by their union with the poor in the community.

Other assistants feel called to live a celibate life in L'Arche, to be thus united with Jesus and with people suffering from handicaps who will never be able to marry. They share their life with them and eat at the same table. By renouncing marriage, their union with Jesus and their desire to serve him at L'Arche in the way of the gospel grows through their relationship with people who are weak. Their celibacy is full of love for people. Other assistants do not feel called to be celibate; they find being single very hard. Through this, they are in solidarity with some of the handicapped people who also find a celibate life hard.

Each assistant has his or her own path. Each is sustained by the presence of people with handicaps and by the union that binds them together. Love, trust and the cry of the poor are the anchors that keep each person on the road of love.

Conclusion

L'Arche communities reveal the paradox presented by weakness and poverty. That which we reject and push aside can become a means of grace, unity, freedom and peace.

Human beings are attracted by success, wealth, power and the limelight, by all that is shiny and big. They reject things that are ugly and poor. By climbing up the social ladder, they become lonelier and lonelier, and increasingly need to defend, hide and protect themselves. They are frightened, and the fear of others often results from a lack of confidence in themselves. They lose a sense of human solidarity, and cut themselves off from the poor. This rejection reveals the shadows, the prejudices and the great poverty of their hearts. But if they can begin to forge links with those who are rejected, they will set out on the road towards freedom.

The Word was made flesh. He hid the glory of his divinity and became one of us. He shared with us his needs, particularly his need for love, and he shared his sufferings. He became poor. He took the downward path and emptied himself to show us a way of communion and love.

At L'Arche we wish to follow Jesus on this path of littleness, humility and trust. We believe that this path is a path of liberation and joy. The spirituality of L'Arche is a way of love and friendship with people who are poor and weak. We are called, in Jesus' name, to live with them a community life that is humble and poor. In eating with them, we discover the beatitude promised by Jesus: "But when you give a banquet, invite the poor, the crippled, the lame, and the blind, and you will be blessed" (Luke 14:13).

In the church, each person is called to live a certain aspect of the life of Jesus. Some, like the apostles, are called to announce the good news throughout the world, others to heal the sick, others to teach, others to shepherd the flock of God. Our role at L'Arche is to live, like Jesus of Nazareth, a simple and poor life open to neighbours and to those who suffer. Jesus lived this hidden life for twenty-eight years. He lived humbly with humble people, ate at the same table as the poor, worked with his hands. And with him in this simple life of Nazareth were Mary and Joseph.

During the public life of Jesus, Mary was scarcely ever present. The apostles surrounded Jesus. But they were not present with him in Nazareth nor at the cross. Then, it was Mary who was close to Jesus. She is the loving, silent, faithful woman who lives in communion and tenderness with Jesus. At L'Arche, we are called to participate in this Nazareth life: to be signs of love in a broken and suffering world. We are also called to participate in the mystery of Mary's compassion for the suffering and rejected Jesus, through being close to people who are crucified, anguished and rejected, people who will never be healed.

Like the Hebrew people travelling through the desert, L'Arche is a people on a journey. We must continue to set out, be disturbed and astonished. After thirty years, we have discovered certain aspects of the gospel that had been hidden to us. Our spirituality, our covenant with the poor is a mystery that we must never cease to contemplate. We must continually set off again, letting ourselves be disturbed by insecurity and led into a new wonderment.

As we continue on our road, we will discover and live other aspects of this mystery, the mystery of Jesus' incarnation, and of the communion we live with him through his hidden presence in the poor.

Future topics in the

L'ARCHE COLLECTION

Personal and spiritual growth – Sue Mosteller

Service: The foot washing – Jean Vanier

L'Arche and the Third World – Robert Larouche

Accompaniment: Journeying together – Claire de Miribel

Ecumenism – Thérèse Vanier

Growth in Spirituality for Assistants and People with Handicaps – Eileen Glass